Pam H

New Zealand in
WATERCOLOUR

First published in 2008 by New Holland Publishers (NZ) Ltd
Auckland • Sydney • London • Cape Town

www.newhollandpublishers.co.nz

218 Lake Road, Northcote, Auckland 0627, New Zealand
Unit 1, 66 Gibbes Street, Chatswood, NSW 2067, Australia
86–88 Edgware Road, London W2 2EA, United Kingdom
80 McKenzie Street, Cape Town 8001, South Africa

Publishing manager: Matt Turner
Editor: Renée Lang
Compilation and design: Denis Robinson

Front cover: Adrienne Pavelka, *Mackenzie Country*, 2005, 35 x 54 cm (detail)

Half title page: Ben Woollcombe, *Mt Peel Station, South Canterbury*, 2006, 33 x 47 cm

Title page (opposite): Alfred Memelink, *Sydney St West, Thorndon*, 2004, 60 x 82 cm

Back page (clockwise from top left):
Jacky Pearson: *Evening Light, Christchurch*, 2007, 50 x 50 cm (detail)
Jan Alldritt-Miller: *Playshells*, Waiheke Island, 1998, 75 x 56 cm
Austen Deans: *Homebush Homestead*, South Canterbury, 1989, 25 x 35 cm (detail)
Gaston de Vel: *Ranunculi*, 65 x 50 cm
Ben Woollcombe: *Kahikatea and Mt Peel*, South Canterbury, 2007, 53 x 23 cm
Paul Hanrahan: *Farmers' Market, Geraldine*, 2008, 36 x 47 cm

National Library of New Zealand Cataloguing-in-Publication Data

New Zealand in watercolour : 30 leading artists paint the country
and its people / Denis Robinson, compiler ; Renée Lang, editor.
ISBN 978-1-86966-194-6
1. Watercolor painting, New Zealand. 2. New Zealand—In art.
I. Robinson, Denis, 1940- II. Lang, Renée, 1949-
758.193—dc 22

10 9 8 7 6 5 4 3 2 1

Colour reproduction by Colourscan (Singapore)
Printed in China through Phoenix Offset, Hong Kong, on paper sourced from sustainable forests.

*To Eugene Fancott,
master of the brush,
man of art, mentor*

New Zealand in
WATERCOLOUR

30 leading artists paint their country and its people

DENIS ROBINSON

Above: Brian Carmody, *Wainui Bay,* Golden Bay, Tasman, 2007, 54 x 74 cm
Opposite page: Ben Ho, *Figure with White,* 2001, 50 x 40 cm

CONTENTS

Above: Ted Sherwen, *Tree Line, Lake Ohau Station,* Canterbury High Country, 1996, 34 x 21 cm

INTRODUCTION

New Zealand, it could be said, was discovered in watercolour. The earliest explorers captured the beauty of the new land in watercolour paints as a way of recording their discoveries. The most notable of these artist/explorers were Sydney Parkinson on Captain James Cook's first ship *Endeavour* and William Hodges with Cook's later voyage on *Resolution*.

The excitement of a country with clear light and lush lands soon travelled to artists in Europe and a succession of them came here from the early 1800s onwards to capture the beauty and subsequently spread the word even further. Among them were well-known names including Earle, Heaphy, Hoyte, Kinder, Gully and Worsely, whose works painted around 150 years ago still endure today, many in such pristine condition that you could swear they were only created in the last week.

Among the early settlers was a watercolour artist of some note, William Hodgkins, who began teaching art in Dunedin in the late nineteenth century with the intention of helping to further the technique among the new communities. His daughter, Frances Hodgkins, went on to become a leading figure in the international art world.

Since those early beginnings, the medium has flourished in New Zealand especially amongst eminent artists such as Rita Angus, Toss Woollaston and Colin McCahon as well as a number of talented amateurs. Each has created in their own way their impressions of their land and its people by way of this most difficult of techniques.

In recent times, however, watercolour works have been generally given a 'back seat' by many of those in New Zealand's dealer gallery world, overshadowed by the currently fashionable and usually more expensive oil and acrylic works. But thankfully some of the most historically important watercolour works are held safely in public gallery collections throughout the country.

There remains some debate among practitioners as to what constitutes the true watercolour technique. The purists would have it that only the original watercolour pigments should be used in a transparent technique (layering translucent colours from light to dark on white paper). However the contenders some find acceptable are acrylic colours, which can be used in both transparent and opaque techniques, and gouache, which is water thinned but opaque in consistency. For the selection process in this book I have generally gone with the rule that the works should be executed in the transparent technique associated with classic watercolour painting, using either acrylic or watercolour pigments.

This has not in any way restricted the variety of creativity and subject matter that you will find within these pages. And it should also be noted that I have not ranked or placed the artists in any order, which aims at giving the reader a nice surprise when turning from one artist's representation to the next, sometimes radically different, style. This selection includes some of the best works from legends in the New Zealand watercolour world to relative newcomers who attempt to push the boundaries of the medium.

Surprisingly, as I discovered in the very early planning stages, this is the first book to present a compilation of the works of currently practising watercolour artists in New Zealand – and what an exciting and pleasurable experience it has been to put it together. But on reading each artist's observations on their work you will find that watercolour has been – and remains – the hardest and most frustrating of media in which to paint.

It should also be noted that there were some artists I approached who, unfortunately, could not get quality images of past work to enable their inclusion. Perhaps next time for them.

I hope that we can all take inspiration from the artists who are featured in this book. I personally think this recognition is long overdue and thank them for their co-operation in making it possible. *New Zealand in Watercolour* should prove to be a valuable reference for art lovers as well as an inspiration to all those people – and they are legion – who enjoy recreational watercolour painting.

Denis Robinson

NANCY TICHBORNE

My involvement with watercolours started with a request to illustrate a cookbook with a strong gardening element, *The Cook's Garden*. This book, a joint effort with my two sisters Mary Browne and Helen Leach, was published in 1980 and was reprinted nine times.

When I was at art school in London watercolours were not taught – they were actually frowned upon! In those days we only worked in charcoal and oils. So when I started on those book illustrations, I had to teach myself to paint in watercolours.

I like the fact that watercolour is by far the hardest medium. It presents wonderful challenges, which I still enjoy after years of watercolour painting. To be in control of its 'waywardness' gives me never-ending pleasure. My portrayal of sensuality in nature is ideally suited to the glorious dynamic of watercolour – the seeping of one colour into another, puddles, run-ons, boundary lines, etc.

I would describe myself as a sensualist – preoccupied by tone and texture, both of which are of course reliant on light. As for subjects, I enjoy an eclectic mix. Flowers, landscapes, faces, cats, gardens, fruit – anything that with the right light becomes magic.

I currently live in French Farm Valley, inner Akaroa Harbour, Banks Peninsula.

Above: *Midday Shadows,* Akaroa, 2000, 34 x 44 cm
This painting was an exploration into the sharp contrasts between very dark shadows and brilliant sunshine. The clarity of light in New Zealand makes our landscape unique. Here all the detail in the shadows has been lost – making an interesting silhouette of the tree trunks.

Opposite page top: *Kowhai and Old Shed*, 1997, 34 x 44 cm
To emphasis the luminosity of the kowhai, I contrasted them with the dark of this old garden on the edge of the bush.

Opposite page below: *Lake Mapourika,* West Coast, 2007, 43 x 54 cm
My work is all about light, which means early morning starts or long waits for the sun to either come out or go in.

Above: *Nikau in Flower, West Coast,* 2006, 45 x 50 cm
Over a period of quite a few weeks, West Coast friends kept us informed on the imminent flowering of this wonderful New Zealand palm. When it happened, we dropped everything to drive across the South Island so I could capture their coral-like beauty. Patterns are all-important in this painting.

Left: *Calendar Girl,* 2005, 25 x 36 cm
Subject matter for me is often spur of the moment, 'stopped in my tracks' happenings and dependent on my camera. Diana, the subject here, was all painted-up glamour, strutting her stuff on stilts to entertain a crowd.

Above: *Sun Lovers*, 2003, 34 x 44 cm
A cat's body language is easy to read, which is probably why so many humans become cat lovers. To see a cat – and a group of poppies – enjoying the winter sun was enough to inspire a painting. It also indulged my interest in the sensuality of texture – cat's fur, crêpe paper-like petals and hairy stems.

AUSTEN DEANS

I first attempted representational painting at the age of 12, drawing the ridges and outline of Mt Torlesse to try to explore how it was made up. I was encouraged by a family friend, Ethel Pyne, a true watercolourist, and on leaving school I enrolled at Canterbury School of Art, graduating in 1939.

I spent six years away from New Zealand, with the army in Egypt as a war artist [during World War II], but was wounded and subsequently became a prisoner of war for four years. On release I returned home to New Zealand to farm work and painting. Some time later I accepted a war bursary to study art in London for two years at London University's art school, after which I returned to Peel Forest in South Canterbury.

With watercolour, I love the ability to quickly cover an area with colour, varying it as you go. Transparency can be very effective in making a good painting, depending a lot on light coming through from the paper underneath. I believe my style to be artistic realism, with my favourite subjects being mountains and bush. I have also had some reasonable success in portraiture in watercolour.

I still live in my home and studio in Peel Forest, and the paintings featured here are all of South Canterbury locations.

Above: *Course of the Potts River,* 2005, 55 x 75 cm
In the mid-afternoon light the snowy-topped hill appears to hover above the curved riverbed shape of the
Potts River as it cuts through glaciated terraces.

Opposite page: *Mid-Canterbury Ranges from Mt Peel Station,* 1992, 80 x 134 cm
I think this is the best of only four I have painted at this size, the largest regular size sheet available.

Above: *Homebush Homestead*, 1989, 25 x 35 cm
My uncle James Deans, who owned Homebush, was a great
rhododendron enthusiast. By luck I arrived to paint Homebush just
when the rhododendron in the foreground was flowering. But sadly
too late for Uncle Jim to see the picture.

Opposite page: *White Deer, Little Mount Peel*, 1992, 54 x 74 cm
When Graham Carr went to Yugoslavia to buy his foundation deer
stock, he was able to buy several white deer which had belonged to
the Yugoslavian Royal Family.

14

15

BEN HO

Born in Canton, China, I studied as a young man at the Canton University Academy of Fine Arts. My works were exhibited in the Fine Arts Exhibition of the Canton District Culture Gallery. In 1988 I emigrated to New Zealand and soon after became a New Zealand citizen.

My father is an artist, and when I was a child he showed me how to draw and paint in the Chinese style. Some years later he arranged lessons for me with his tutor, a Chinese style master, who eventually said to me: 'In the future it won't matter how good you become; you will still recall my style, so you must go out and draw and study from real life.' I am glad I followed his instructions.

At university in Canton, I would spend anything from 15 minutes on a loose study, drawing from memory, up to 100 hours doing a detailed study. It was a very good but, at times, a very boring way to learn.

I studied the European Old Masters and the Impressionists, and did a lot of experimental painting from real life, and eventually I understood how to mix and use colour in my own painting style.

I now hold many teaching classes of my own and my works have been purchased by collectors in New Zealand, the USA, the United Kingdom and Australia.

I have recently moved to live near Queenstown.

Above: *Sparrows on the Window,* 2000, 53 x 75 cm
The likes of this old barn, where sparrows always come around to visit, can be seen anywhere in New Zealand.

Opposite page: *Fishing,* 2002, 46 x 52 cm
This painting was painted from memory. It will always remind me of the days onboard, spent fishing with friends.

Above: *Irises*, 1996, 51 x 74 cm
Flowers have always been my favourite subject in watercolours. Especially with large-size works like this one.

Opposite page: *Sea Breath*, 2003, 46 x 52 cm
This painting catches the sound of a sea breeze. It is just one example of the music of nature.

JANET ANDREWS

I first painted with watercolour high up in the mountains, in Canada, while on a course with a well-known Canadian landscape artist. I haven't stopped painting since.

Watercolour can be a frustrating medium, but at its best it has a translucence, a glow, that no other application of colour can match. This is particularly apparent in J.M.W. Turner's English watercolours – it is said that watercolour was his favourite medium.

As for the other (often listed) characteristics of watercolour, they are at the same time both the challenge and the reward. The colours hit the paper running – they may separate, granulate, form hard edges where the water leaves them high and dry – the element of surprise hangs over each work until the bitter end. It is not possible to paint a good watercolour without confidence and a certain carelessness, a 'big picture' approach, establishing the light underlying the whole, then revisiting the dark and the detail.

I suppose landscapes and seascapes appeal to me most as subject matter, though I do enjoy painting figures. I look for patterns and layers, folded and eroded landforms, waves and currents in water, repeating cloud shapes. I am striving for simplicity, a cleanness of both paint and composition.

I live and work on the shore of Wellington Harbour, at Days Bay.

Above: *Waterfall,* Fiordland, 2007, 76 x 56 cm
Needless to say I painted *Waterfall* after a trip to Fiordland. In the haziness the scene abstracted itself – scattered light, glimpses of edges, the deep dark of fiord walls.

Opposite page: *Harbour Patterns,* Wellington Harbour, 2004, 56 x 76 cm
On calm days the harbour is often covered by patterns, like secret rivers flowing under the still grey surface.

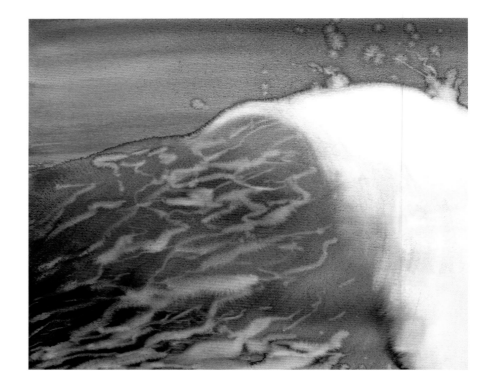

Left: *And Still the Centuries Flow By,* Aoraki Mt Cook, 2003, 130 x 56 cm
Mountains, rivers and gravel … components of an endless cycle. This work resulted from 10 days spent walking the tracks in the Mt Cook region. Playing on the translucence of the watercolour, it is backlit by being encased in laminate and mounted in front of a light box.

Above: *Wave,* Wellington Harbour, 1998, 56 x 76 cm
The mesmerising action of waves breaking is surely something we have all experienced in our days on the beach … the slow stretching of the patterns on the curving face before the inevitable collapse.

Opposite page: *Flight,* Pauatahanui Inlet, 2005, 56 x 76 cm
This painting is one of a series depicting the inlet. It is less about this particular bird – a Royal Spoonbill, rather ungainly and comical on land, but sheer elegance in the air – than about the idea of flight itself.

23

JACKY PEARSON

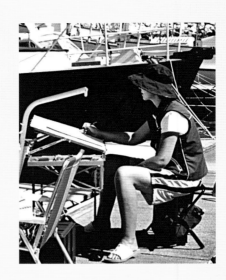

I am fascinated by light and atmospheric effects, which are the driving force for me to paint.

For many years I painted with oils, but have now become totally committed to the transparent effects of watercolours. Using a wet-on-wet and impressionistic *alla prima* approach, I find that watercolours provide the mood, sense of freedom and spontaneity that I aim to convey in my work. I love painting streets full of life, but I keep coming back to maritime scenes as I have lived with boats since I was a child. I make design sketches and do a draft painting on site, then complete the painting in my studio.

I received my early art training in the UK and held my first solo watercolour exhibition in Eastbourne in 1994. Before that, in 1991, I moved with my family to New Zealand. Other solo exhibitions have included 40 paintings representing the complete series of New Zealand's classic coastal lighthouses. The paintings were subsequently turned into a series of three successful calendars.

In 2007 I was chosen to represent New Zealand in the permanent collection of Mexico's National Museum of Watercolours. I am a member and regular exhibitor of Watercolour New Zealand.

Above: *Around the Harbour, Wellington,* 2006, 56 x 76 cm
There are so many facets of the harbour that I want to capture. These three distinct vantages (Petone Wharf, Evans Bay and Eastbourne Coast Road) on one large sheet were quite a challenge!

Opposite page: *Milking Time, Horowhenua,* 2007, 45 x 76 cm
I have always loved the look of these flat, loamy, productive fields seen on SH1 during our frequent trips north. Usually we are travelling at 100 km/h but finally we had the time to stop and really look.

Left: *Commuters, Wellington Railway Station*, 2007, 32 x 20 cm
Rain has a wonderful way of connecting shapes, and I couldn't resist this human mass putting their 'brollies' up and dashing to their places of work.

Above: *Old Timer, Rangitikei*, 2007, 30 x 20 cm
This historic 1850s cottage is happily under the care of the local restoration society in Ohingaiti. The painting came out of a fun weekend painting with members of the Watercolour New Zealand society.

Opposite page: *Evening Light, Christchurch*, 2007, 50 x 50 cm
Christchurch is a wonderful place to paint; it's full of lovely old buildings that throw long shadows across the streets.

DON DONOVAN

I started using gouache as a studio boy when I was 15. But it wasn't until 1985 that I started to make watercolours when I was asked to illustrate *New Zealand Odyssey*, for which I did the drawings and text and Euan Sarginson took the photographs. I did over 700 watercolours for that book, of which about 170 were used.

Since then I have written and illustrated several books with subjects covering old pubs, old houses, old general stores and a collection of New Zealand country churches. My illustrations were also used extensively by *Historic Places* magazine.

Pen and watercolour is my preferred medium because it's quick – I don't think I've ever taken more than an hour to complete a watercolour. It's an unforgiving medium; you can't do much repair; but it also benefits from its spontaneity, some interesting unforeseen effects and the charm of mistakes revealed – dodgy perspective being my hallmark.

I like architectural subjects; mostly old ones. I particularly like distorted weatherboards and lichen-encrusted masonry. There's a certain honesty about early New Zealand structures that you don't see too often these days.

I live on 10 acres at Albany, north of Auckland, and all of my books and watercolours have been produced in my large studio/office. I've had a privileged life.

Tui Brewery, Mangatainoka

Above: *Tui Brewery, Mangatainoka*, Wairarapa, 1995, 19 x 27 cm
This work appeared in my book *The Good Old Kiwi Pub* as a secondary illustration on the spread devoted to the nearby Dudley Arms.

Opposite page: *Deconsecrated Roman Catholic church, Raukokore*, Eastern Bay of Plenty, 2001, 18 x 25 cm
A sketchbook rendering, no more than 10 minutes in the making, this exhibits a satisfying impulsiveness; I made a more formal painting from it later. The note I made under the drawing at the time reads: 'The deconsecrated R.C. church at Raukokore that the police raided and found packed to the rafters with pot!!' The drawing appeared in my book *Country Churches of New Zealand*, published in 2002.

Left: *Old St Pauls, Wellington*, 1995, 30 x 21 cm
St Pauls, a Gothic structure designed by
Frederick Thatcher, was built in 1866. I
painted this illustration when planning the
book that was finally published as *Country
Churches of New Zealand*. St Pauls, being a city
church, was not included in the book.

Above: *Railway Barrier, Woodville*, 1996,
34 x 18 cm
Every part of this automated pole gate
is necessary to its function; I found it
fascinating because, to me, it was nothing
short of public sculpture, practical sculpture
that also moved and made ringing noises!
The detail was a delight to draw.

Above: *Wains Hotel, Dunedin,* 1996, 30 x 36 cm
I'm seduced by the intricacies of Victorian architecture and fortunately Dunedin's city fathers have made a better job of preserving it than those farther north. This illustration of the 1879 'Italianate' hotel appeared in *Historic Places* magazine.

WARWICK RUSSELL

As a student I had excelled in art classes, having been blessed with a natural talent for illustration. I pursued art at secondary school and followed up with evening classes. In 1960 I established a graphic art studio in Sydney and ran it for three years, during which time I was invited to join the 'Black & White Club' art group. This group had well-known illustrators and cartoonists such as Clem Seale, Tony Rafty and Eric Joliffe among its members.

My OE took me to London and Europe and included a summer in the eastern Mediterranean sailing, sketching and painting. Then I moved on to the Caribbean and Florida. Arriving back in New Zealand in 1964, I started my own graphic studio but by 1998 computers had taken over so I decided to concentrate on the enjoyment of serious watercolour painting. I turned my woolshed into an excellent studio, which became the meeting place for a small group of like-minded people who met weekly. We called ourselves 'The Woolshed Art Group'. Since then I have had some success in art exhibitions.

The spontaneity of watercolour gives the feeling of positive attitude to my work, with a freshness and strength of colour and with fast direct expression.

With my yachting and farming background I am happy painting seascapes, landscapes and old buildings. I live in rural Whitford, South Auckland.

Above: *The Brookby Blue Gum*, Auckland, 2005, 35 x 28 cm
Painted in great haste as many sandflies helped themselves to my bare legs as I sat on my farm bike.

Above: *The Scow Rahiri*, 2006, 36 x 26 cm
Referenced from a black-and-white photo in the book *Phantom Fleet* with the following caption: '*Rahiri* loading stock at Tryphena Harbour, Great Barrier Island, 1906'.

Above: *Twilight Cowshed,* Clevedon, 2004, 53 x 36 cm
Created to record the remnants of old-fashioned hard work involved in dairy farming in the 1950s, appropriately located in Twilight Road, Clevedon.

Left: *Scow Dandy racing in 1905 Auckland Regatta,* 2006, 24 x 36 cm
Referenced from a black-and-white photo in *Phantom Fleet* by Ted Ashby. As a young boy I remember the old scows plying the coast and waterways of the Tamaki and Clevedon Rivers.

Opposite page: *A-Class Keeler, Tawera,* 2007, 35 x 27 cm
I had raced against *Tawera* in the late 1960s so painting her brought back great memories.

ADRIENNE PAVELKA

After 21 years as a graphic artist and illustrator in Christchurch, a fortuitous meeting with Bill Braden, owner of the Yukon Gallery in Whitehorse, Canada, saw the start of my new career and love affair with 'fickle' watercolours.

My early paintings comprised a limited tentative palette and a detailed style. Then a watercolour workshop in Ashburton with dear Austen Deans gave me an appreciation of the landscape and a shove in the right direction. My current style, which has changed and evolved over the years, is to eliminate the detail and simplify and emphasise the effects of the sky's rhythms and light on land or reflected water. I now prefer to work on site at every opportunity or from line-and-wash sketches. I use a big brush and gallons of pure colour to achieve a clean, fresh effect.

As well as challenging me, watercolour creates its own unexpected (and sometimes awful) surprises, but the elation of successfully meeting the challenge is very satisfying. I prefer to paint intuitively and deliberately ignore rules and theories – it's riskier but much more fun.

Lyttelton is now my home and it's where I have a studio/gallery overlooking the ever-changing harbour. I have bellbirds, fantails, a very elderly fox terrier and a very tolerant husband for company.

Left: *Mackenzie Country,*
South Canterbury High Country,
2005, 35 x 54 cm
Early one July Anne Murray of Glenmore Station, Lake Tekapo, invited Paul Deans and me down for a few days' painting. I remember having to stand on a cushion to paint as my feet were freezing and a southerly was imminent. The high-country colours of purple, cobalt blue, dragon's blood and gold capture the permanence and character of the land and its steadfast people.

Opposite page: *Across Grove Arm,*
Marlborough Sounds, 2005,
35 x 52 cm
A still winter afternoon in Marlborough's Ngakuta Bay with the low sun creating clear, glorious deep blue and green reflected shadows.

Above: *Mesopotamia,* Canterbury High Country, 2004, 30 x 50 cm
A happy weekend painting with friends up the Rangitata River valley and hosted by Ann Prouting of Mesopotamia Station.

Left: *Avon/Heathcote Estuary,* Christchurch, 2007, 34 x 62 cm
Another big nor'west sky over Pegasus Bay. I offset the soft flowing effect and colours of the sky with hard-edged tide lines.

Opposite page: *Amuri Area,* North Canterbury, 2004, 30 x 52 cm
Painted from a sketch and colour notes done on the way home after tutoring at the Amuri Autumn Art School at Hanmer Springs.

BRIAN CARMODY

I've been painting in watercolour since 1948 and still have plenty to learn about this fascinating and seductive medium. Although I've worked in other media, I've always returned to watercolour and can truthfully say that I haven't yet mastered this engrossing and often infuriating paint. Sometimes it does what I want it to, often it does not, and it was some years before I learnt to let the paint have its own way and for it to lead me on to make a more satisfying and stimulating picture.

I am still discovering what I like to paint about New Zealand, but have had great satisfaction from coastal places, lakes and rivers, and have only recently discovered Fiordland with its luminous and changing clouds and water. I am drawn at present to visit inland river valleys, but know that I will always return to former themes of water meeting land. To travel overseas is to see one's own country with greater clarity and feeling. I have learnt a lot from visits to China and that place, if any country, may have had some influence on my work.

I have no idea how to describe my style of painting, if I have one. I paint what I enjoy looking at and feel about in the most satisfying way I can at the time. To analyse my work is for others to do. However, if I can communicate through my paintings the beauty of New Zealand, maybe some viewers will work to save it.

Above: *Hydro Lake Reflections,* 2006, 41 x 35 cm
The links between sky and water and the resulting reflections are always interesting.

Opposite page: *Catlins Coast,* Otago, 1996, 54 x 74 cm
Wide coastal views are an integral part of New Zealand shorelines.

Above: *Summer Showers,* Wellington Harbour, 2005, 54 x 74 cm
The harbour has endless combinations of light, cloud, rain and mist.

Above: *Wainui Bay,* Golden Bay, Tasman, 2007, 54 x 74 cm
Late afternoon sun and reflections always appeal to me.

WENDY MASTERS

I grew up in Silverstream in the Hutt Valley and have a Design Diploma in Graphics from Wellington Polytechnic.

I was inspired to try watercolour at a workshop run by Kapiti artist Tui MacLauchlan who used the paint in a free and creative way that appealed to me. I love the paint itself – the way the colour moves in the water and settles as it dries, the subtleties of unlaboured washes, and the glow of the white paper shining through. There is not much room for correction – patience, snap decisions and courage are required! I paint mainly from the subject, concentrating on the rhythms of light and shade, colour and form which are of the essence at that moment, inside or outdoors, still or living.

My use of line drawing with watercolour washes allows the paint to be tone and colour (which often flow from one object to another) while the line picks out detail or broad shapes, often independently of the paint. I'm interested in the different sorts of line made by brush, pen, oil pastel and especially conté chalk drawn into wet paint.

I live on the Kapiti Coast north of Wellington.

Above: *Farm Camp*, Coromandel, 1996, 54 x 70 cm
This is an enlargement of a small painting done at Whangapoua Beach. I used a brush and waterproof black ink followed by simple washes.

Opposite page: *Waihi Picnic*, Coromandel, 2006, 54 x 72 cm
This family picnic in the reserve was a colourful drama in the pohutukawa shade, and the beach a sunny backdrop. I painted as fast as I could and finished it later from a photo.

Above: *Field at Riverside,* Martinborough, 2002, 27 x 38 cm
I've often painted this field of old cabbage trees near Martinborough – it looks like a desert in drought years, but this time it was a soft green summer.

Opposite page: *Valley Road, from the Raumati Escarpment,* Kapiti Coast, 72 x 54 cm
I took a photo while climbing the hills above Paraparaumu and painted this at home, drawing with a conté chalk into the wet paint.

SUSAN HARRISON-TUSTAIN

My mum and dad nurtured and encouraged my creativity from an early age. To begin with, I painted in oils and was particularly inspired by the rich depth of colour and evocative lighting captured by Rembrandt. In 1991, during a visit to Europe, I was so transfixed by the ability of watercolour to portray light that I decided to try painting with this luminous medium and to see how far I could take it.

Subsequently I evolved my own style of 'naturalistic realism' and an unconventional technique of using watercolour emerged – inspired by the multi-layered oil painting methods of the Old Masters.

Inspiration comes from so many things around me and I am constantly seeking to learn, improve, challenge and grow. My subjects range from flowers to figure studies to still lifes to birds and beyond, but each painting is not so much about subject or technique. I want my work to say something – there needs to be a reason for a painting's existence. I want my work to reach out of the frame and connect with the viewer so that the memory of the painting will stay with them long after they leave its presence.

Living in the countryside overlooking Tauranga and Mount Maunganui, I find my home and studio provide a feeling of sanctuary for my paintings to emerge and take flight on their own journey.

Above: *On Active Service*, 2001, 26 x 40 cm
This is a painting of pride, love, and nostalgia. The letter speaks in a self-effacing way of the writer being rewarded for his actions, but also hints at some of the difficulties he's experiencing. It's a painting I felt driven to create. It was a pleasure and an honour to portray a symbolic tribute to all those who served.

Opposite page: *The Wind's Song*, Mount Maunganui, 2007, 109 x 49 cm
There is a tense, almost electric atmosphere as the storm passes. Gulls are brightly lit against the leaden sky. I wanted to evoke their cries as they were carried away on gusts of September wind at my local Mount Maunganui Ocean Beach. Elements of John Masefield's poem 'Sea Fever' inspired this painting: 'The flung spray … the gull's way … and the wind like a whetted knife.'

Left: *The Sentinel,* Akaroa, 2007, 42 x 21 cm
Keeping a watchful eye over his domain, a New Zealand kingfisher quietly surveys the Akaroa Harbour. The commercialism of the sign on which he is sitting is dulled as nature quietly spreads her cloak again.

Above: *Curious?* Wairarapa, 2006, 25 x 14 cm
Are you drawn to look inside? I was. After 20 years of passing by this little Wairarapa church I finally took the time to experience the treasure trove of kauri pews, vaulted ceilings and glorious stained-glass windows behind these unassuming doors.

Opposite page: *Home is the Sailor,* Tauranga, 2003, 31 x 24 cm
This is a work that speaks of one man's lifelong and historic connection with seafaring. The point of conjunction of light rays hints subtly at his association with the Port of Tauranga – the sailor's safe haven. Home at last.

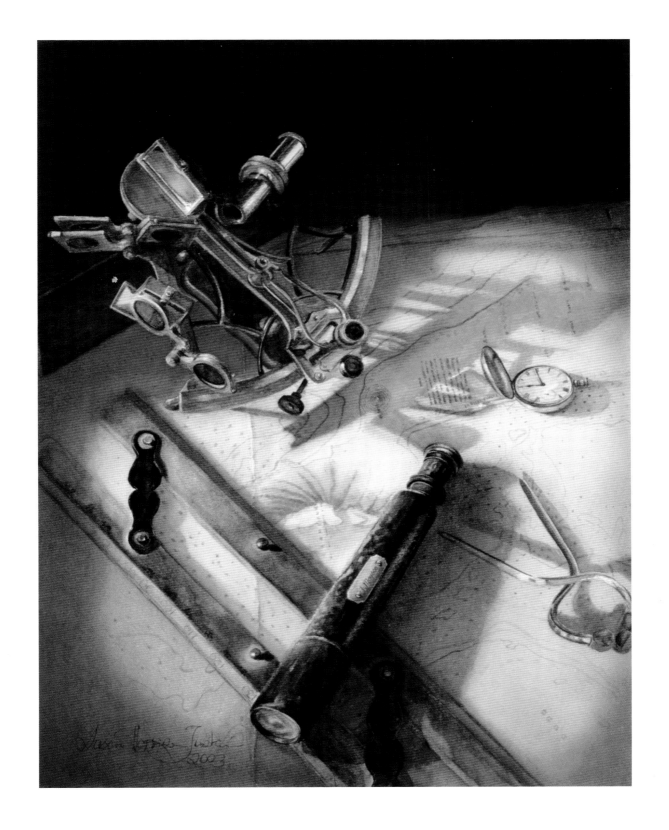

PAUL HANRAHAN

I happened upon an art book in the early 1960s that really appealed to me. The paintings in it had an impact, spontaneity and freshness that belied the sombre palette. That the medium was watercolour began to interest me. I held the usual perceptions that watercolour was a wishy-washy medium done by provincial art society members and a poor relation to oil painting.

How wrong I was. I looked to the art of Homer, Wyeth, Seago and the beautiful watercolours of John Singer Sargent to set about coming to grips with this cantankerous medium. I was certain it was going to suit

my impulsive nature. With lengthy perseverance the terrifying white paper soon became friendlier. Laying wash over wash didn't suit – too slow, so one day in a fit of pique, I slashed almost pure pigment onto paper. I was now getting somewhere using less water. Now I paint strong colours side by side in one wash where I can, and try to leave some of the paper white to give the picture sparkle.

My painting can be categorised as 'figurative impressionism' – narrations of people doing things in everyday life.

I now reside in a place that overlooks the buzzy South Canterbury town of Geraldine and is located not far from some of New Zealand's most notable artists.

Above: *Tug at Timaru Port,* South Canterbury, 2008, 36 x 54 cm
'Unauthorised persons prohibited' and other barricades seemed to block any chance of a good subject on this particular morning. When I saw these vessels, I decided to become an 'authorised person'.

Opposite page: *Rendezvous on Colombo,* Christchurch, 2003, 25 x 42 cm
Where people gather I'm compelled to draw. Here the café entrance in cool shadows contrasts with sunny outdoor dining.

Above: *Peonies at Craigmore,* South Canterbury, 2007, 36 x 54 cm
As I sketched at this imposing estate west of Timaru, the peonies and elegant old stable came under my pencil. I particularly liked the random structure at left.

Opposite page top: *Farmers' Market, Geraldine,* 2008, 36 x 47 cm
Tents and umbrellas popped up like mushrooms. The interaction of young and old, dressed up and dressed down, makes my painted snapshots of life worth doing.

Opposite page below left: *The Green Bach, Rangitata,* South Canterbury, 2008, 27 x 36 cm
This subject said 'holidays the way they were'. Farm bikes with vertical salmon rods appeared in almost every yard.

Opposite page below right: *Steam at Pleasant Point,* 2007, 27 x 36 cm
This little South Canterbury town boasts a small but wonderful steam rail adventure fuelled by enthusiastic hobbyists. The control box and church steeple make a good composition.

ROBIN KAY

I have a lifelong commitment to watercolour. When I was 10 years old I won an English magazine competition (the name of the magazine was *Meccano*). The prize, sent out from England, was a set of Winsor & Newton artist-quality watercolours and a block of watercolour paper.

Then, while still in my teens, when my family was living in Gisborne, I used to go with a couple of friends on watercolour painting trips at weekends under the private tuition of Eric Gully (the great-grandson of John Gully).

During my final school year in Christchurch, I attended on a part-time basis painting and drawing classes at the Canterbury University College School of

Arts. I experimented later with oils, but to me they lack the translucency and the challenge of watercolour.

My favourite subjects are landscapes, seascapes and the built environment. I paint in response to the beauty and drama of the world around me. I aim to capture the effect of light on the land and on water and in the sky. My painting style has evolved over the years. It ranges from the representational to the impressionistic.

The frustration with watercolour is that if you make a mistake halfway through it can be very difficult to lift it out. Often you just have to start the whole painting again. But that is when the speed of execution is an advantage. When it comes off, the spontaneity gives the painting life. I now live in Wellington.

Above: *Boatsheds, Paremata, Wellington*, 1987,
30 x 53 cm
My wife, Barbara, and I lived for some 30 years
at Pukerua Bay and we would frequently drive
over the bridge at Paremata. The reflections of
these boatsheds were often magical.

Right: *Before the Regatta, Paremata*, 1987, 26 x 55 cm
The 'yachties' are preparing to sail on the
Pauatahanui Inlet during their Easter Regatta.
The strong colours of the sails contrast with the
dark velvet of the wet sand.

Opposite page: *The Three Sisters, Tongaporutu,
Taranaki*, 1997, 36 x 54 cm
The outermost of these rock formations near
the mouth of the Tongaporutu River has since
eroded away – so they are now two-and-a-bit
sisters!

Above: *West Coast Beach, Mabel Bay,* 1967, 35 x 45 cm
In the summer of 1966/1967 my family and I drove down the West
Coast of the South Island. The sculptural forms of huge pieces of
driftwood have always interested me. This was painted on the spot
at Mabel Bay.

Opposite page: *On Mount Ruapehu, Tongariro National Park,* 1977,
37 x 55 cm
I have painted the majestic mountains of Ruapehu and Ngauruhoe
many times. The blueness of snow in some lights reminds you that it
is frozen water.

ROBIN KAY 1977

59

TED SHERWEN

I was fortunate to gain a place as an apprentice lithographic artist with a large publisher in the early 1950s in Glasgow, Scotland. A few of the artists were excellent fine arts painters. This was my first serious introduction to fine arts/design, later enhanced by the design class at the Glasgow College of Printing, then the Stow College of Printing. I was taught to paint by Californian Rex Brandt, National Academy of Design, American Watercolour Society. (He was on a different page!)

The directness of watercolour had instant appeal for me. Do not be fooled by its tag: 'a simple medium'. Simple can be complex in transparent watercolour.

I paint with a fairly broad approach, any whites are white paper preferably painted round. My aim is to marry content/subject with formal fine arts design elements/form. I seek a total surface. Many paintings start with an amalgamating soft-edged underpainting, which offers a give-and-take relationship with the subject. This can be up to mid-tone in strength and can allocate linked whites or passage of colour which is woven through the painting. I 'borrow' from local colour, but always select a palette deemed appropriate to the subject and my goal.

Subject matter must interest me and have good shape/pattern potential. A painting is good because it feels good, not because it looks good.

PREFERS TO WALK. SHERWEN 2004

Familiar Faces
Omahanui
T. Sherwen '97

Above: *Familiar Faces, Omahanui,* 1997, 52 x 35 cm
Omahanui is a garden at Greenhithe, Auckland, which used to be open to the public over a very short period each November. This is a nice mix of local colour, people, plants and bush.

Opposite page: *Prefers to Walk,* 2004, 41 x 29 cm
Most mornings I walk through a small wetland where pukekos are regulars; they are about as daft as humans. This watercolour is a result of observation over many kilometres and many grey dawns.

61

Above: *Tree Line, Lake Ohau Station*, Canterbury High Country, 1996, 34 x 21 cm
Composition by four flat overlapping washes that were kept quite abstract and allowed to dry each time. Pencil work was added after wash No. 3. The final wash, thalo green, was allocated 60 per cent of the subject.

Left: *This Sporting Life,* 1991, 72 x 54 cm
This work started life as a bold geometric landscape. I frowned and washed it out by sponge. The damp surface was selectively aggravated with a Steelo pad. The rugby players were painted on direct – no drawing. One of the few that over many years I have actually been quite pleased with.

Above: *The Way Time is Told, Brighton Beach,* Christchurch, 1999, 74 x 54 cm
The Velasquez-style low-key palette was augmented with cobalt blue to give added resonance to the
greys, which suited the austerity and integrity of Brighton Beach.

GARRICK TREMAIN

Having worked in a wide variety of occupations I decided, in my late twenties, to aspire to the life of an artist or writer. I was living in England at the time and so I sought commissions to produce pen drawings of country homes. I quickly proved I could make a comfortable living with just a little acumen and my right hand.

Competent in line, I had a desire to work in colour, to paint, in other words, so I added wash to my pen drawings. As my confidence grew, the penwork was abandoned and I found myself as a watercolourist.

The medium held appeal for me as a viewer. The translucence of light reflecting from the paper, rather than from the paint surface of opaque media, is much of its charm. As a painter I delight in its capricious nature; the 'happy accidents' that eventuate when fluidly applying water and pigment. Its frustrations come when working outdoors in the southern winter, my favourite plein-air season: paint that appears to have dried while still in the field can thaw and run from the paper in the warmth of the car or studio.

In subject matter I am particularly drawn to old buildings and the reminders men have left of their time in the landscape. When I moved into the Wakatipu Basin in 1971 there were many such subjects. There are fewer now, but the light and the markedly differing seasons remain a special gift.

Above: *St Bathans, Central Otago*, 2007, 36 x 54.5 cm
This ghost of a once-populous mining town now sports just one hotel and a handful of residents. However, a steady stream of visitors trickles through this picturesque village perched above the famous Blue Lake.

Opposite page: *Hotel Cardrona, Central Otago*, 1995, 23 x 51 cm
A building little changed externally from its early days (once a hotel, now a restaurant). In the 1960s the publican would ration the intake of drivers depending on which way they were travelling: the gentle road to Wanaka or the hazardous zigzag to Queenstown.

Above: *Home Straight,* 2000, 35 x 47 cm
From the age of seven I have had a love of thoroughbred racing. This is one of many experimental treatments of a spectacle that has long set my pulse racing.

Left: *Celmisia, Wakatipu Basin,* 1987, 19 x 28 cm
The celmisia daisy is a favourite subject when it makes its summer appearance. When I first moved to the Wakatipu Basin it spread in wild carpets beside dirt roads that have now become sealed roadways with featureless mown verges.

Above: *Baiters, Westland*, 1980, 36 x 44 cm
On this occasion I had slept in my van beneath dripping kahikateas. In the morning fog there were the sounds and shapes of whitebaiters on the water. The image stayed with me until I reached my Wakatipu studio that evening.

BRIAN MILLARD

My first box of Winsor & Newton watercolours was given to me when I was a child. This wondrous black box with its pans of mysterious and exotically named pigments was in constant use for many years, setting me on a journey that is still in progress.

I like a challenge and watercolour is a major challenge. I like its immediacy, its convenience and its surprises. It makes demands on concentration and focus. It is totally unforgiving yet will reward you generously, sometimes when you least expect it.

I fit loosely in the Impressionist category; style emerges after a while without encouragement, you can't manufacture it. Style is relative to the method one uses. My preference is for the wet-on-wet method where soft edges predominate, and where accidents are encouraged and retained.

I tend to think in terms of shape, value, pattern, mood and colour. As a result anything can spark my interest. It is all to do with light. If I am excited by something, an effect of light perhaps, then for the moment that is my favourite subject.

My partner, the watercolourist Marilyn Palmer, and I live near Arrowtown in Otago where we have our studios and gallery.

Above: *Snowline,* Otago, 2008, 30 x 99 cm
This painting was inspired by the intriguing snow patterns of the peaks of the Harris Range along the Matukituki Valley. I was fascinated by their strong graphic content and stark counterchange of both value and colour.

Left: *Mist Rising, Lake Wanaka,* 2007, 54 x 120 cm
Early morning on the west side of the lake. I hope I have captured the peace of this perfect spot.

Above: *Dart Station,* Otago, 2008, 64 x 98 cm
On the road to the Routeburn Track there is a backdrop of peaks that can be seen from Dart
Station and Routeburn Station and which offer an endless variety of painting opportunities.
Here I have juggled a few minor elements, and exaggerated the light on the edge of the
midground trees. The sheep serve to add interest, but the jagged mountaintops are the heroes.

Above: *Mt Earnslaw and Turret Peak,* Otago, 2008, 64 x 99 cm.
I have painted spectacular Mt Earnslaw many times. Each time I do, I see more and learn more. There always seems to be snow at some level. The mood changes constantly. In this winter scene I have tried to capture the grandeur of the mountain by simplifying and underplaying the midground and by keeping the foreground soft and out of focus.

Opposite page top: *Last Light Crown Range,* Otago, 2008, 64 x 98 cm
Late afternoon is a good time to drive over the Crown Range.

I have often been rewarded with memorable images bathed in 'magic light'. There is a sense of looking through rose-coloured glass. The sheep, painted *contre jour* or against the light, are on or near Glencoe Station.

Opposite page below: *The Rees River,* Otago, 2008, 30 x 99 cm
The Rees and Dart rivers feed Lake Wakatipu from beyond Glenorchy. In autumn the banks take on a distinct golden hue due to the profusion of willows and poplars. This is an impression of the time and place painted from memory.

PETER COATES

I've accepted the challenge of watercolour for over 60 years. I was lucky as a child in that my father worked for a firm that imported Daler-Rowney watercolours, giving me the chance to experiment with the wonder of the medium, which I have loved ever since.

I suppose I would classify myself as an 'expressionist painter' in that I try to express the emotional reality of a subject rather than its physical reality. To achieve this I use all watercolours and many internal symbols – colour, texture, veneers, calligraphic lines, splatter, dribble … the lot. I am continually experimenting with what can be achieved in the medium, and I am inspired by the work of Turner and the French-Irish landscape watercolourist Louis Le Brocquy.

Among the many strengths of watercolour are its encouragement of spontaneity, its transparency, its fluidity, its ability to express atmosphere and movement, its link with calligraphy. Its weaknesses are its tendency to fade, the high cost and fragility of framing, limitations of size and limited textural effects.

My subject matter reflects the diversity of my life – my family life, my television experiences, New Zealand life and landscape, my love of travel, and of music and poetry. I live and paint in Wellington.

Above: *Family Under the Christmas Tree*, 1998, 55 x 70 cm
A painting inspired by our family ritual of opening presents under the tree on Christmas morning, with my wife Annie, our two children and other friends' children.

Opposite page: *From Houghton Bay, Wellington, Looking to the South Island, Sunset*, 2006, 55 x 70 cm
The sunsets across the Kaikouras are always an inspiration to me along my favourite part of the Wellington coastline.

Above: *Courtenay Place in the Rain,* Wellington, 2004, 65 x 95 cm
At night Courtenay Place is alive with people and with colour. This is especially true when it's raining and the coloured
lights of the bars, restaurants and traffic are reflected on the drenched roads. As the crowds mingle with the lights, the energy
of the night is enhanced by movement. This was painted on location and in my studio from photographic reference.

Above: *Crowd Leaving the Stadium After the Game,* Wellington, 2005, 65 x 95 cm
I have experienced the scene here on many occasions and in many different moods. Much depends on whether the Hurricanes win or lose, but so often coming out into a cold southerly with a crowd of twenty or thirty thousand after an exciting match contrasts greatly with the mood in the stadium when you watch the game. This was painted in the studio from a series of photographic references.

JAN ALLDRITT-MILLER

I have drawn and painted all my life. In the late 60s I developed intolerances to many foods and my beloved oil paints.

I envisaged an easy transfer to watercolour. This beautiful but elusive medium proved immensely frustrating, but the struggle led me on a fascinating experimental journey using acrylics as watercolours. I felt like a pioneer, as at that time I could find no one else in New Zealand who was using them in this way. Acrylics allow me to glaze over previous washes, whilst still achieving the wet-on-wet techniques of traditional watercolour.

I use only eight tubes of paint; no white, no black, and adore the three 'graining' colours: burnt umber, ultramarine and alizarin – and the exciting nuances of colour achieved by mixing them.

My style of painting is representational. I love painting and recording nostalgic vignettes of life – discarded rural memorabilia, forgotten buildings, deserted rail tracks and stations, hidden garden corners, personal moments. Textures inspire me, too – rusty metal, lichen-covered wood, stones, soft flower petals and foliage.

Part of my week is spent teaching in Auckland, the rest at my Sandspit (near Warkworth) gallery/studio. I also love travelling around the country conducting intensive two-day painting workshops.

Above: *Granny*, 2006, 36 x 26 cm
I drew this woman, the mother-in-law of a dear friend, six weeks after she'd had a mastectomy at the age of 95. Knitting, without glasses, she confided she had no energy for digging her vege garden at present! She brought up a family on a farm, in dense bush country with no road access. A once-yearly event was to travel by paddle steamer down the Whanganui River to the city.

Above: *Crinolines*, 1999, 65 x 90 cm
Unhappy with this work, I left it sitting for several weeks on my studio table. Then I spilt some dark paint
on the top portion – that was the answer! I reworked the darks behind the flowers to push them forward.

Left: *Retired,* Horopito, 2006, 59 x 41 cm
Horopito is one of my favourite places – an artist's paradise, where the movie *Smash Palace* was filmed and where there are acres and acres of rusting, lichen-covered vehicles and their skeletons. The more treasured ones had made it into sheds. When last I visited, this shed had collapsed on the car.

Above: *Changing Perspective,* Aramoho, 2005, 75 x 56 cm
I had hoped one day to live in Wanganui. Sadly, circumstances changed and the dream faded. As I sat at the abandoned Aramoho station, struggling to draw the changing perspective of the track, it seemed a metaphor for my life which I also view with a 'changing perspective'.

Opposite page: *Playshells,* Waiheke Island, 1998, 75 x 56 cm
This work was developed from an on-site sketch of my daughter Wendy. She was an adult before I finally did the painting.

Above: *One Rainy Evening on Oriental Parade*, Wellington, 2007, 60 x 82 cm

Oriental Bay, the Riviera of Wellington, is often portrayed in sunshine but is equally inviting in any weather. When it rains or a southerly is blasting a path through Wellington, one's normal reaction is to venture out in the open for the least time possible – umbrella up and head down. However, this is also the time when the city comes alive in a new way and presents a stunning show that can thus so easily be missed. Magnificent vibrations of light and colour from buildings and traffic form a brilliant dance as they are reflected in the huge mirrors of the wet streets.

Above: *Southerly Storm, Houghton Bay*, 2006, 40 x 60 cm

Wellington is bounded by a magnificent, enormously varying coastline – from the protected harbour with its sheltered coastline and beaches to the wild, moody and fully exposed south coast. The area acts as a mecca for those who love the sea and feel at one with it. Houghton Bay with its big surf and tight but exposed bay is one of the popular attractions along the scenic south coast.

Above: *Winter Shadows, Upland Road,* 2007, 40 x 60 cm
Winter presents Wellington city in a wonderful new atmosphere of cool sunlight sneaking in at low angles and casting lovely long and interesting shadows. The crisp and clear low winter light creates exciting tones and contrasts, presenting inspiring moody atmospheric scenes just waiting to be painted.

BEN WOOLLCOMBE

My earliest inspiration to paint came while watching Austen Deans painting on the Ball Glacier and later peering into his studio and becoming almost drunk on the smell of turps and linseed oil. During the 1970s I experimented with watercolour and was entranced by the way it enveloped the page, forming passages of light and dark at great speed.

In 1977 I had my first solo exhibition of watercolours at the Durham Gallery in Auckland, followed by many others, showing work from the South Island and many world trips.

Watercolour painting is greatly suited to travelling and plein-air painting, it involves carrying the least amount of equipment and affords great mobility. Often the best view is a scramble up a bank or mountain! Watercolours have a certain immediacy and charm almost unattainable in other media.

I'm a literal painter, although on close inspection it's all an illusion coming together as a coherent image viewed from a distance. I paint a lot of landscapes as these are the true wonders in a land of rather dull architecture and drab dress, but at any time I can be inspired by a composition regardless of subject.

I live in Peel Forest, South Canterbury, amidst the deeply folded foothills of the Southern Alps.

Above: *Formerly 'The Blackball Hilton', West Coast, 2006, 35 x 52 cm*
When you come into Blackball you can't miss the grand 'Old Lady' near the top of the street. After a letter from the Hilton Hotel chain's lawyer, the name of this hotel had the word 'formerly' added to avoid legal proceedings!

Opposite page: *Kahikatea and Mt Peel*, South Canterbury, 2007, 53 x 23 cm
Mt Peel is an icon of South Canterbury being bush clad and visible from afar. Painting late in the day offers some very dramatic lighting and colour.

Above: *Evening Over the Rangitata River*,
South Canterbury, 2006, 41 x 75 cm
The dark shadows of the foreground
contrast well with the warm light
tones of the sky and middle distance.

Far left: *Bodhi*, 2007, 74 x 49 cm
While visiting Bodhi, good friend,
painter and sculptor, we got out the
wine and brushes. A very brisk work
painted with oodles of water was the
result.

Left: *Teapot and Mug*, 2000, 26 x 37 cm
Some days when it's raining a still life
indoors makes for a good subject.

Above: *Mt Peel Station*, South Canterbury, 2006, 33 x 47 cm
After a good snow, warm willows and the trim of the old cottage contrast well with the deep cool shadows. Sunlit snow always makes for dramatic lighting, which I have painted here very broadly with lots of water and a large squirrel mop brush.

SUE WICKISON

Following a four-year degree in Scientific Illustration, I spent nine years as a botanical illustrator with the Royal Botanic Gardens, Kew. While other painting media were taught at university, watercolour was the traditional medium for this particular genre of meticulous illustration and it certainly has been the tradition at Kew – and worldwide in botanical art for the last few centuries.

I have used watercolour techniques in the field to record colour notes of plants before they (the plants) were pressed for collections. The luminosity of watercolour and the fine nuances of delicate colour changes are part of the appeal to me and yet layers of controlled dry brushwork can sharpen and add a stronger depth of paint and impact.

Watercolour has been my preferred medium for 30 years and one that still challenges me as an artist. It is a medium that I am still learning and which maintains the excitement of each new painting. Capturing the minute details of texture and colour differences is a passion of mine. All natural history topics interest me, in particular botanical subjects.

I hope that my art helps to record the exquisite beauty of nature, opens viewers' eyes and passes on a smile. I live and work in the Ohariu Valley, Wellington.

Above: *Pohutukawa in Full Bloom* or *Scot's Pohutukawa*, 2005, 72 x 50 cm Iconic to all New Zealanders, these vibrant red flowers conjure up memories of the beach, summer and Christmas. The fine detail of this work, the size of the painting and the sheer coverage of paint on the paper took over three months to create.

Above: *The Colour of Time,* 2007, 50 x 50 cm

This was the first of my more contemporary botanical paintings and the pohutukawa leaves shown here in
a clock format depict the passage of time. From the young pale green leaf to the dried grey leaf at 11 o'clock,
the audience likes to guess which leaf represents them on the Clock of Time.

Above left: *Flax Flowers, Phormium tenax*, 2006, 100 x 40 cm
Movement and colour are the two main qualities that I wanted to capture in this painting of the striking flax flowers that can be seen standing tall above the strap-like leaves in summer.

Above middle: *Smiles of the Pohutukawa*, 2007, 80 x 20 cm
The pohutukawa has many different coloured smiles that can be spotted by looking closely at or beneath this tree which has become such an icon to most New Zealanders.

Above right: *Kowhai, Sophora tetraptera*, 2006, 80 x 20 cm
The fresh yellow of the kowhai heralds spring and is a favourite of many birds. The picture captures the various stages from the young lime-green buds through to the textured dried seed pods.

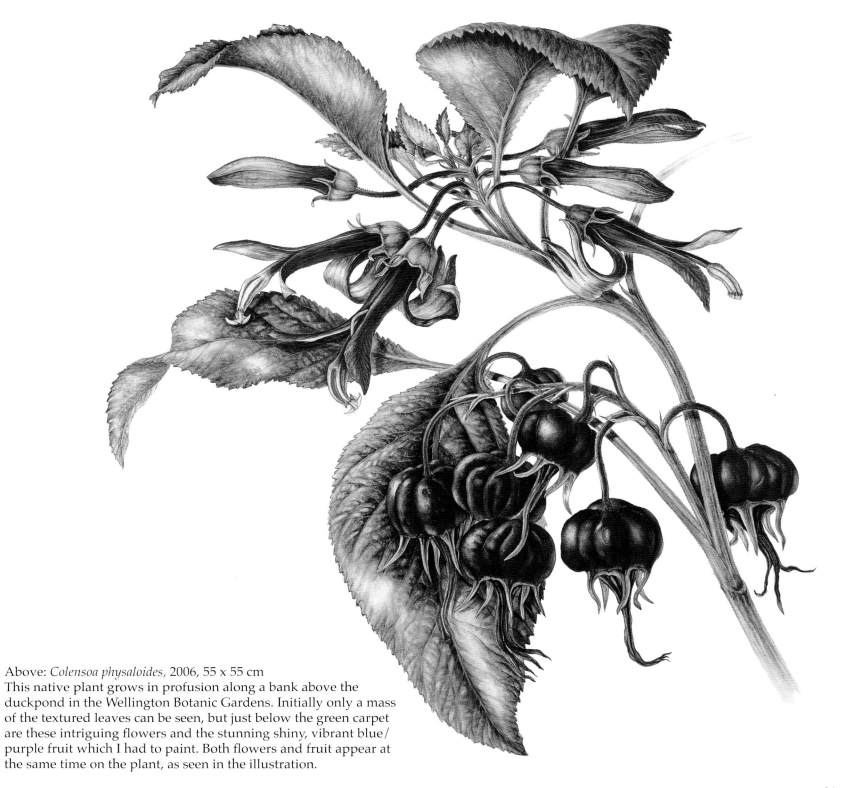

Above: *Colensoa physaloides*, 2006, 55 x 55 cm
This native plant grows in profusion along a bank above the duckpond in the Wellington Botanic Gardens. Initially only a mass of the textured leaves can be seen, but just below the green carpet are these intriguing flowers and the stunning shiny, vibrant blue/purple fruit which I had to paint. Both flowers and fruit appear at the same time on the plant, as seen in the illustration.

ANGUS WATSON

Quite some time ago I read a book that had been recommended to me on the American painter Charles Reid and I liked it so much I rang him and subsequently spent a week in Mendocino at a watercolour course he was taking. His method was loose, bright, very painterly and a style I was taken with. Just an idea of attaching the shadows to the background and letting the colours have their head and splashing on the water.

On the way to the United States I discovered the work of LeRoy Neiman and realised that if I used the density of colours and painted the shadows, then I could be free to use any colour, not just the real colour, and somehow the image would still work. The idea is to make sure I've got a good combination of colours and then the image should slowly unfold. I have to base the painting on something, but after that the subject is secondary to the colour.

I love the spontaneity of watercolour and the way that things happen unexpectedly. I like to give the paint a chance to surprise me – and if it's all a total disaster, then I start again and do it quickly, hoping to capture that spontaneity and get it right.

I would describe my style as impressionistic – loose and colourful. I admire the Japanese approach of aiming to keep it simple: one hour to think about it, one minute to do. My home and studio are just out of Queenstown, below Coronet Peak.

Above: *Lost Love*, 2007, 75 x 56 cm
My favourite model who, sadly, has now gone.

Above: *Cattle Muster*, Central Otago, 2007, 55 x 76 cm
I was forced to stop this painting before I could overcook it because some people came in and bought it before the paint was even dry.
Then I had to frame it – and away they went and I was left wondering if I had even done it.

Above: *Fleur's Place,* Moeraki, 2004, 55 x 75 cm
We visited Fleur's Place in Moeraki after a happy weekend
exploring on the Otago coast. As expected it was wonderful,
slightly off-the-wall and as quirky as its creator Fleur Sullivan
who, in a previous incarnation, founded Olivers Restaurant in
Clyde. The food at Fleur's was delicious, too!

Left: *The Commodore,* Lake Wakatipu, 2007, 56 x 75 cm
Jay helped organise a traditional small boat regatta on Lake Hayes
to raise funds to restore the old boat shed at Frankton on Lake
Wakatipu. A sunny afternoon and about 25 small boats made a
spectacular day.

Above: *Really!* 2006, 55 x 80 cm
I had an idea for a painting of bright, loose, almost caricature-type images; simple figures at a cocktail party. I got the first two down easily and thought I would use the girl next door to model for the third figure, She became a mission to capture and although I did get her in the end she slipped out of the caricature department into another. It still worked, though.

RAYMOND RAMSAY

I began painting in watercolour as the result of a challenge from a workmate early in my career as an illustrator. Until that point I had focused on media such as acrylic and oil and during a studio discussion someone said I would never master watercolour. Not being the type to take this lying down, I promptly set out to prove them wrong and discovered a lifelong love of watercolour along the way.

The technical challenge and the intricacies of watercolour are one of the things that make it interesting to me; the translucent nature of the medium is exciting to work with and I enjoy manipulating it to achieve results not readily possible in other media.

Stylistically I am probably weighted towards the traditional; however, my approach is more often dictated by the essence of my subjects. I choose things to paint depending on what takes my interest and often subjects that evoke a sense of history or have an interesting story to tell. Of course the New Zealand landscape and climate provide plenty of stimulation as well.

I currently live and work from my studio in the hills above Palm Beach on Waiheke Island. I have had a long history with the island and enjoy both the painting and the fishing that is on my doorstep.

Above: *White Rock Reef,* Wairarapa, 2006, 11 x 23 cm
The wind was on the rise over this old fossil reef as a storm was on its way, making the seas quite turbulent with the spray flying about wildly. I took the opportunity to paint while I could and got some reference down on paper.

Above: *The Old Anzac,* Waiheke Island, 90 x 140 cm
This craft had been in Anzac Bay for so long it had almost become a fixture, and the dilapidated seagull-strafed hull made a great subject.
I thought of the seas it had resisted that were now getting their revenge by breaking it apart and settling it to its resting place.

97

Above: *Towards Mercury Island,*
Coromandel Peninsula, 1999, 49 x 71 cm
This was sketched while I was fishing in
the Coromandel: the cloud formation of
a coming blow with the sea changing in a
rising wind and smashing onto the rocks
below. It was painted later in my studio out
of the squall.

Left: *Pauatahanui Inlet*, Wellington, 2007,
10 x 20 cm
On my way out of Wellington I took
the back road through the top of the
Pauatahanui Inlet. I looked left to
Plimmerton township and was caught
by the colour of the storm-laden sky, the
light catching the green hills and the Inlet
entrance with the township set out in relief.

Above: *Jim Whispers' Dream,* Waiheke Island, 1999, 40 x 56 cm
My attention was caught by the shape of a hull and the rust colour catching light amongst the mangroves in a part of the Rangihoua Creek.
On investigation I discovered the two hulls and was told by the owner of the property they were built by Jim Whispers. Jim was apparently a
little eccentric, but he had a dream to build a boat and sail on an adventure. The hulls were made from a variety of materials gathered at the
local tip. Needless to say it never sailed, but Jim had built his dream and I could not resist painting it.

MURRAY STUART

I have always had an interest in art. On leaving school I trained as a signwriter. Then, while I was in America on signwriting business, I took the opportunity to spend a week with a top American watercolour artist and discovered the beauty and magic of watercolour.

I believe watercolour more than any other medium demands skill in drawing, brushstrokes, colour and design but, once mastered, it gives great satisfaction. It is a bit like golf; just when you think you have it beaten, it turns and bites you. For me, that's part of the appeal of watercolour, the challenge is always there for the next masterpiece.

My style of painting is influenced by my background. I love using brushes, so my brushstrokes are sure and bold, and my colours are clean and bright. I love loose and spontaneous paintings. Expression rather than imitation is my aim.

My favourite painting subjects – seascapes and boats – stem from a background of competitive and recreational sailing. I also love the challenge of street scenes and cityscapes.

I work mostly from my home and gallery in Arkles Bay, Whangaparaoa, but my paintings and workshops take me around the country and beyond. Even though I paint in other media, watercolour will always be my passion and medium of choice.

Above: *On the Slipway, Okahu Bay,* Auckland, 35 x 52 cm
Most people wouldn't give this boat at Okahu Bay a second glance but to an artist it is a perfect subject. This painting follows the vignette formula as taught by American artist Ed Whitney.

Opposite page: *Sandhills,* 2008, 35 x 54 cm
There is a strong feeling of contrast in this painting: the whiteness of the sand against the dark of the grasses. Warm against cool, dark against light – all key to a successful work.

Left: *Durham Lane*, Auckland, 2006, 35 x 25 cm
Inner-city streets with their fascinating lights
and shadows are always fun. The challenge is
to interpret and simplify the scene. I have used
a limited palette for this painting.

Opposite page: *Arkles Cliff*, Whangaparaoa,
2007, 25 x 35 cm
This quick and spontaneous painting was done
at Arkles Bay where I live. The ever-changing
colours of the trees and cliff face always beg to
be painted. These 'on the spot' paintings are
often the most successful, this one in particular
as it won first prize at a local art exhibition.

GASTON DE VEL

If you were to ask me I would say that watercolour is the most difficult medium to use. I trained in oils at the Académie Royale des Beaux-Arts in Brussels, but after three years I felt that I had become stale. So I tried aquarelle (transparent watercolour) and discovered a bright new world in which to play.

One of my most influential tutors was Alfred Bastien, a former winner of the Prix Godecharle and friend of Claude Monet and John Singer Sargent. I believe I am one of the last painters to have been taught in the classical and impressionist fashion by a tutor directly involved with some of the leading artists of that movement.

After I established myself as a professional painter in New Zealand, I began painting in an impressionist style and have interpreted lively scenes of sun-drenched courtyards, fishing ports and geranium-filled cafés, all affording New Zealanders a welcome glimpse of exotic locations. I was awarded the Kelliher Art Prize in 1968.

I enjoy plein-air (on location) painting and try to travel for a period each year, looking at colourful subjects in many corners of the world.

I live in Orewa on the Hibiscus Coast north of Auckland.

Above: *Ranunculi*, 65 x 50 cm
Because of its likeness to a bunch of wildflowers, a subject par excellence, not sensational but perhaps just the poor artist of wildflowers.

Above: *Reclining Nude*, 1988, 40 x 30 cm
A classic subject. And a good test to see if I get the flesh tones right, a never-ending problem for many artists.

Left: *Motorcycle,* 1980, 65 x 50 cm
An attractive subject for a younger audience
– and me, too.

Below: *Old Boots,* 1987, 21 x 27 cm
Another interesting challenge to find out what
can be done with a simple subject.

Opposite page: *Purple and Yellow Tulips,*
60 x 45 cm
These contrasting colours make a stunning
tribute to spring. In watercolour you can never
go wrong with flowers, with freshness being
the order of the day.

JUDITH TREVELYAN

It was the paper that first attracted me to watercolour over oils and acrylics. I love the clear white of the paper and decide quite early on which areas are going to stay untouched. Sometimes I leave quite a lot of white and sometimes just a tiny bit, but it's always a very important part of the painting. I don't like using masking fluid, either – I really need to see those lights while I'm working.

It's a great feeling spreading wet paint over a clean sheet of paper – sometimes it all falls apart, but when it works it's really satisfying. Of course, the downside is that you just can't mess around with watercolour – but that enforced directness is one of the most pleasing things about a successful watercolour. It's hard to put labels on different styles of painting, but I suppose mine could be described as 'realistic' or 'traditional', though I hope my paintings show a bit more excitement and interest than that would suggest.

I've lived and worked in Wellington most of my life and while I've been lucky enough to travel extensively, I'm always inspired by subjects close at hand. I've painted many portraits and still lifes and return to familiar landscape subjects in Kelburn, in Thorndon, at Makara and on the south coast again and again. I'll never run out of interesting subjects while I live in this visually exciting city.

Above: *Sydney Street, Thorndon*, 1998, 56 x 60 cm
Historic Thorndon is a favourite part of Wellington for artists and these cottages in Sydney Street have been painted many times. I wanted to find a less familiar angle and this view is from Kelburn Park.

Opposite page: *Upland Road, Kelburn*, Wellington, 2000, 56 x 56 cm
I live just around the corner from this subject and have always loved the long shadows that stretch across the road here.

Above: *Days Bay,* Wellington, 1998, 56 x 75 cm
Days Bay, on the eastern side of Wellington Harbour, is surrounded by bush that comes down almost to the beach. I tried here to get the feeling of the bay without having a painting dominated by green.

Left: *Fishing Boats, Ngawi,* Wairarapa, 1999, 56 x 75 cm
This was painted on the spot on the sloping beach at the isolated fishing village of Ngawi on the south Wairarapa Coast. The tractors and boats were so complicated and my position so wobbly that I just let rip and aimed at capturing something of the generally busy and colourful atmosphere.

Opposite page: *Jug on the Table,* Wellington, 2000, 56 x 75 cm
This is my own backyard – a perfect mix for me of still life and landscape.

Right: *Occidental Bar, Vulcan Lane*, Auckland, 2008, 60 x 40 cm
The Occidental Hotel on Auckland's Vulcan Lane at 5 pm on a Friday evening. The buildings had a wonderful warm hue to them, all the colours I love to use.

Opposite page top: *Little Waihi*, Bay of Plenty, 2007, 30 x 50 cm
An example of truly original Kiwi baches, where people just walk out of their back doors to their own jetty. Painted on site, quite a tricky subject for this.

Opposite page below: *From the Shore*, Auckland, 2007, 60 x 80 cm
This is a wonderful view of Auckland city viewed from the North Shore with its contrasting low tide and mangroves. To make this painting easier I used a very limited palette, which lent itself to the late afternoon light.

JOHN RUNDLE

I started painting about the time I left school in the late 1940s. At first it was pen and wash, but soon I was doing straight watercolours. Oils came later and gouache later still. I entered watercolours in the National Bank Awards and won a merit and a special prize. After a period of rejection I started having my paintings, mostly watercolours, accepted for other exhibitions such as those of the New Zealand Academy of Fine Arts.

There is great satisfaction in producing a successful watercolour. It is as big a challenge as climbing a mountain or crossing a pass, but the failure rate is high and a watercolour is not as valued by the uninformed public as other media. In the museums and public galleries they are not even called paintings; they are drawings. The artistically aware know better.

I suppose my style would be described as figurative although there is a lot of memory and invention in them. My core subjects are mountains as that is where I have spent much of my time. I live on the Western Hutt hills above Petone.

Above: *Lambton Quay*, 1995, 70 x 100 cm
The canyon-like streets of modern cities provide many interesting compositions that are challenging to paint. Wellington is especially exciting because as well as the older parts of the city, there is the central area of high rises crowded into a small area by the waterfront.

Opposite page: *Mt Ruapehu*, Central Plateau, 2007, 35 x 55 cm
The mountain seen here at the end of the long straight road leading from National Park towards Ruapehu. This whole area has a great variety of country that provides many different types of subject from forest, to desert, to alpine.

117

Above: *Mt Angelus,* Nelson Lakes National Park, 1999, 32 x 51 cm
This peak is near Lake Rotoiti. It is a pleasant and easy mountain to climb and there are extensive views from its summit of the lakes and mountains of the Travers Range. This is the view from Hukere Stream that we saw shortly after leaving our campsite. Later that day we climbed the mountain from the right.

Left: *SAR (Search and Rescue),* 2005; 34 x 43 cm
For many years I was involved in mountain search and rescue. This is a typical occurrence – a helicopter slowly comes in to land on a tiny flat in a narrow bush valley. The crewman is talking the pilots down, giving them information on nearby trees and other obstructions while the search party waits on the edge of the flat to be picked up.

Above: *Sparrow,* 2007, 27 x 37 cm
I met this bird at Raglan. I invented a world for him in watercolour and created him in gouache. These two media work well together and can create interesting effects.

AVIS HIGGS

My father, Sydney H. Higgs, was also a watercolour painter who learned painting from his Tasmanian grandfather and uncle, both of whom were called Joshua Higgs.

I learnt to paint initially from my father and I was sketching in watercolour from the age of 12. After leaving school I attended Wellington Art School and then worked as a commercial artist.

During World War II I was in Sydney where I worked as a textile designer and continued to study painting in the studio of Desiderius Orban. After the war I took a collection of textile designs to England and worked there until 1952 when a car accident forced me to return to New Zealand. I have now been painting in watercolour for over 75 years and continue to enjoy creating new paintings. I have enjoyed painting bush and water scenes and experimenting with new ideas.

I like watercolour because an idea in my mind can be expressed quickly and immediately. I am probably an impressionist painter and like the speed of creating a watercolour that allows me to finish before my idea has changed.

I now live on the side of the Wadestown hill in Wellington and I continue to enjoy painting the views of the harbour, city and the ships in the port that can be seen out of my studio window.

Left: *Sherry River,* Waimea County, Nelson, 1965, 73 x 55 cm
This painting is of the river that has colours to match its name. It was included in an exhibition at the Centre Gallery in Wellington, which was opened by the Queen Mother in 1966. It was quite an honour to be introduced and to talk to the Queen Mother about my paintings on display, including this one.

Above: *Deserted,* Sherry Valley, Waimea County, Nelson, 1963, 57 x 46 cm
Sherry Valley is near Tadmor, south of Nelson, where I spent a number of painting holidays with my father.
This painting received the National Bank Art Award in 1963. It is now held in the National Collection in
Te Papa, Wellington. (Avis Higgs/Museum of New Zealand Te Papa Tongarewa (1964-0023-1))

Above: *Under the Grapevines*, 1953, 48 x 38 cm
This was painted at the house of Katherine Phillips near Nelson. The house was originally owned by Katherine's parents and in the nineteenth century they would board people overnight on their way to the West Coast goldfields.

Above: *Bay of Islands*, 1970s, 64 x 50 cm
This was painted while I stayed with artist friends Huia and Fassett Burnett who lived in a beautiful bay in the Bay of Islands. It is one of a number that I painted at the time and which reflect the moods of the area.

JOHN KEITH REED

My earliest interest in art began in England where, as a child, I drew 'boys' things' such as boats and aircraft. This provided an excellent grounding in line and tone. My parents nurtured my passion and, after moving to New Zealand and settling on the Otago Peninsula, I discovered that the light and moods of this idyllic setting with its wild seas and stormy skies, its foggy mornings and driving rain could best be captured through the spontaneous effect of watercolour. I held my first exhibition, a sell-out, at the age of 16.

While studying for a degree in Fine Arts at Canterbury University I became aware of the significance of Impressionism and Expressionism in a more global world of art. I experimented in abstract oils and favoured the Cubist movement, which influenced my watercolour work as well. My work became more suggestive and gestural, looser and not overworked.

A sponsored trip to Europe in 1996 provided fresh subject material; from the charm of French villages to the grand architecture of the cities, from the canals of Venice to the fishing ports of southern England. Such places with their softer lights and sense of history have had a major influence on my more recent work.

Now living in rural Marlborough, I work from my studio/gallery at home. Visitors are welcome, by appointment.

Above: *Cambridge,* Waikato, 2004, 40 x 56 cm
I painted this because of my fascination with the trees and their canopy effect, similar to that in Arrowtown.

Opposite page: *French Farm,* Banks Peninsula, 2004, 55 x 76 cm
This larger painting shows a more panoramic view of some of the bays around Banks Peninsula. My interest was to play with the smoke from the nearby cottages. We stayed in the red-roofed cottage.

Top: *Havelock from the Marina*,
2004, 40 x 56 cm
Seen from sea level, this view
provided me with a variety of
interesting elements from the
cottages up on the hill through
to maintenance activities on
the boats in the foreground.
An early morning topic with a
magical atmosphere.

Left: *Te Mata Hills*,
Hawke's Bay, 2004, 55 x 76 cm
The attraction to paint this
subject was the side light and
the soft shadows, along with
the up, down nature of the
winding road. The hills add
a solidity to the foreground
landscape.

Right: *Vulcan Lane,* Auckland, 1991, 56 x 40 cm
A must-do painting of this well-known Auckland spot. The older forms of architecture and the squeezed-in shopping area have a parallel to European market areas. The objective was to capture the 'looking up the lane' composition along with flashes of colour from signs and figures.

CONTACT DETAILS

ARTISTS INCLUDED:

Jan Alldritt-Miller, Treetops Gallery, 1042 Sandspit Road, RD2 Warkworth 0982. Mob 027 498 7676, email: janalldrittmiller@yahoo.co.nz, website: www.janalldrittmiller.com

Janet Andrews, Southlight Studio, 614 Marine Drive, Days Bay, Lower Hutt 5013. Ph 04 562 7200, email: janet@southlight.co.nz, website: www.southlight.co.nz

Brian Carmody, 43 Bidwill Street, Mount Cook, Wellington. Ph 04 384 6523, email: dorothy.carmody@xtra.co.nz

Peter Coates, 121 Rakau Road, Hataitai, Wellington. Ph 04 970 2115, email: ap.coates@paradise.net.nz

Austen Deans, Te Omanga, Peel Forest, RD22 Geraldine 7992. Ph 03 696 3574

Don Donovan, PO Box 300-136, Albany, North Shore 0752. Ph 09 415 9701, Mob 027 383 5598, email: donovan@ihug.co.nz, website: www.donovansworld.blog.co.nz

Susan Harrison-Tustain, 85 Castles Road, Oropi RD3, Tauranga. Ph 07 543 3933, email: susan@susanart.com, website: www.susanart.com

Paul Hanrahan, 18 Downs Road, Geraldine 7930. Ph 03 693 9750

Avis Higgs, 2 Wadestown Road, Thorndon, Wellington. Ph 04 473 6346, email: familysteel@paradise.net.nz

Ben Ho, 51 Alec Robins Road, Lake Hayes, Queenstown. Ph 09 483 9368, Mob 021 272 1098, email: benho.art@xtra.co.nz

Robin Kay, 94 Ellice Street, Mt Victoria, Wellington 6011. Ph 04 973 4388, email: totaranui@paradise.net.nz

Wendy Masters, 208A Manly Street North, Paraparaumu Beach. Ph 04 902 4182, email: jeremymastersnz@yahoo.co.nz

Alfred Memelink, PO Box 33327 Petone. Studio/gallery Ph 04 568 5869, Mob 021 472 156, email: alfred@memelink.co.nz, website: www.memelink.co.nz

Brian Millard, 493 Speargrass Flat Road, Arrowtown. Ph 03 442 0932, email: watercolourworkshop@ihug.co.nz

Bernadette Parsons, Franklin. Ph 09 232 6889, Mob 027 555 1169, email: cbparso@ihug.co.nz

Adrienne Pavelka, 1 Crossland Terrace, Lyttelton 8082. Ph 03 328 9598, email: paveldov@clear.net.nz, website: www.adrienne-pavelka.com

Jacky Pearson, 230 Muritai Road, Eastbourne, Wellington. Ph 04 562 8664, email: jacky.pearson@watercolours.co.nz, website: www.jackypearson.com

Raymond Ramsay, Titoki Road, Palm Beach, Waiheke Island. Ph 09 372 9094, email: raymond@rsramsay.com, website: www.rsramsay.com

John Keith Reed, PO Box 2, Spring Creek, Marlborough. Ph 03 570 5520, email: jkreed@xtra.co.nz, website: www.artworks.co.nz

John Rundle, 64 Maungaraki Road, Korokoro, Petone 5012. Ph 04 589 1658, email: janrun10@clear.net.nz

Warwick Russell, Whitford Park Road, RD1, Manurewa 2576. Ph/fax 09 530 8678, email: warwickrussell@ihug.co.nz

Ted Sherwen, Ph 09 489 6193, Mob 021 666 193, email: tedsherwen-watercolours@xtra.co.nz

Murray Stuart, 2 Cochrane Avenue, Whangaparaoa 0932. Ph 09 428 0170, email: murraystuart@xtra.co.nz

Nancy Tichborne, 104 French Farm Valley Road, RD2 Akaroa 7582. Ph 03 304 5678, email: tichborne@watercolours.co.nz, website: www.watercolours.co.nz

Garrick Tremain, 188 Domain Road, RD1, Queenstown. Ph 03 409 8244, email: tremain@queenstown.co.nz, websites: www.garricktremain.com, www.garricktremain.co.nz

Judith Trevelyan, 33 Grove Road, Kelburn, Wellington 6012. Ph 04 475 7046, email: trevelyan@xtra.co.nz

Gaston de Vel, 31 Forest Glen, Orewa. Ph 09 426 6540, email: develart@ihug.co.nz, website: www.internationalartcentre.co.nz

Angus Watson, 355 Littles Road, RD1, Queenstown. Ph 03 442 8486, email: guswat@queenstown.co.nz, website: www.anguswatson.com

Sue Wickison, Aranmore, 924 Ohariu Valley Road, Ohariu, Wellington. Ph 04 478 5090, email: sue@suewickisondesign.com, website: www.suewickisondesign.com

Ben Woollcombe, 136 Blandswood Rd, Peel Forest, RD22 Geraldine 7992. Ph 03 696 3890, email: bensart@xtra.co.nz, website: www.benwoollcombe.com

AUTHOR:

Denis Robinson, 76 Scott Road, Whangaparaoa 0932. Ph 09 428 5301, Mob 021 425 638, email: denis@artdirection.co.nz, website: www.artdirection.co.nz